emoji moon

haiku and related text

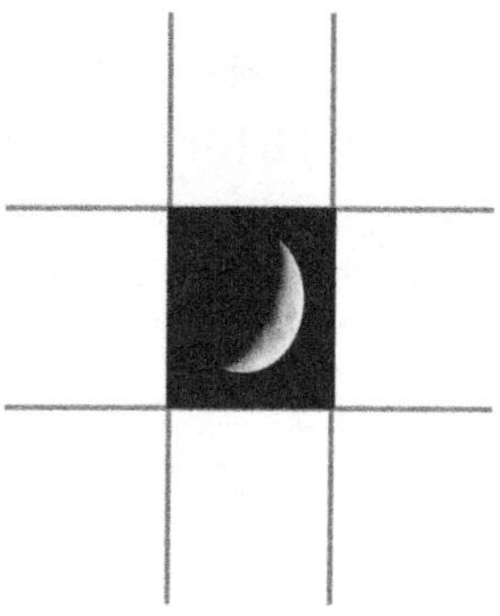

JOHN STEVENSON

emoji moon

Published by
Red Moon Press
P. O. Box 2461
Winchester VA
22604-1661 USA
www.redmoonpress.com

Cover Art: Beatrice Gaudreau, *Untitled*
Acrylic on cardboard, 2018.
By permission of the artist.

Second Printing

We live in our description of reality.

— *Gregory Bateson*

Foreword

"Don't tell me the moon is shining; show
me the glint of light on broken glass."
> — *Anton Chekhov*

This quote, which is probably familiar to many of you, is most likely a poetic summary of Chekhov's writing advice in a letter to his brother in 1886. His actual advice included examples and specific directions. I take some small comfort in knowing that even Chekhov had some difficulty simply showing his reader "where to look," rather than clearing a path to the destination! I am not a haiku poet; I am a playwright and director.

In theater, as in haiku, we are told, "Show, don't tell." We trust in the intelligence and imagination of those who experience our words, hoping that each individual will actively participate in the discovery of meaning — and, by doing so, add additional levels of possibility to our original intent. In my artistic world, I can do this in multiple ways — through carefully constructed revelations about character, plot and theme over the course of a 90-minute production. The signposts in haiku are far more subtle — a raised eyebrow in the direction of a moment in time. Haiku infers, indicates, suggests.

Emojis are also a kind of shorthand statement, but any statement followed by a smiley face, a pile of poop, or a series of little pink hearts makes it clear exactly how our words are to be interpreted by the audience. No inference is needed or allowed. (It seems important to mention here that I have never known John to use an emoji!) And the moon? Symbol of mystery, subtlety, and change, it's powerful presence defies our attempts to reduce it to anything less than itself. The light it gives is wholly reflected from another source. And, even then, Chekhov advises us to come to see the moonlight by its effect on the smaller [broken] things around us.

One of the best things about being in love with a writer is that I get to be surprised and moved, again and again, by the ways in which the moments of his solitary life, and our lives together, show up on the page. For me, some of these may be "emoji moments;" an event I believe can be summed up in one simple, emotional response (usually mine!). And then I'll read a haiku from John's perspective about the same moment, for which I happened to be present.

her soup making
fills the apartment
autumn evening

And I can see the glint of moonlight.

— Michael Kennedy
September 2018

emoji moon

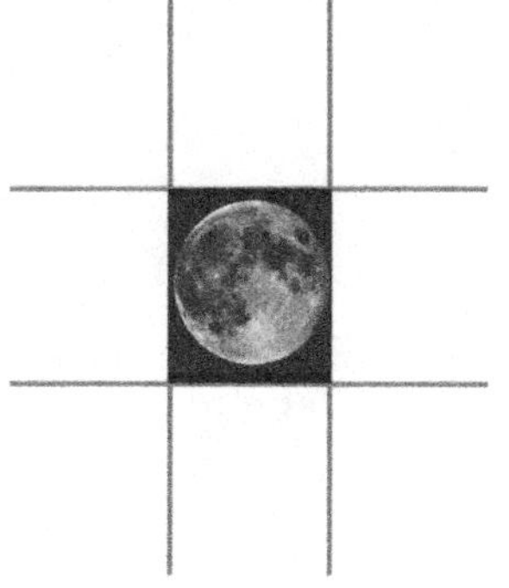

dawn
gathering
a quorum

WHY HAIKU

There are so many of us. If even a small part want to be heard it seems only fair to be brief.

> a lakeside
> weekend . . .
> mayflies

stick figures
including one
i recognize

winter trees
how small
a small town gets

fresh snow
sadness for
the old sadness

in
love
the
in
visible

if glass breaks easily a bird

teeth going beyond

winter mountain
in the conversation
as a listener

feeling strong
this morning,
I could go on
getting uglier
another thirty years

thin green
as if we
never happened

leafing out
that part of the world
we drive through

junk car
the hum of bees
beneath the hood

in duckweed
    a channel
full of stars

waiting room
we all look up
as the rain arrives

They're sending
someone over.
I don't know who.
Someone blue
to sky it all up.

estate sale
the hard
erasers

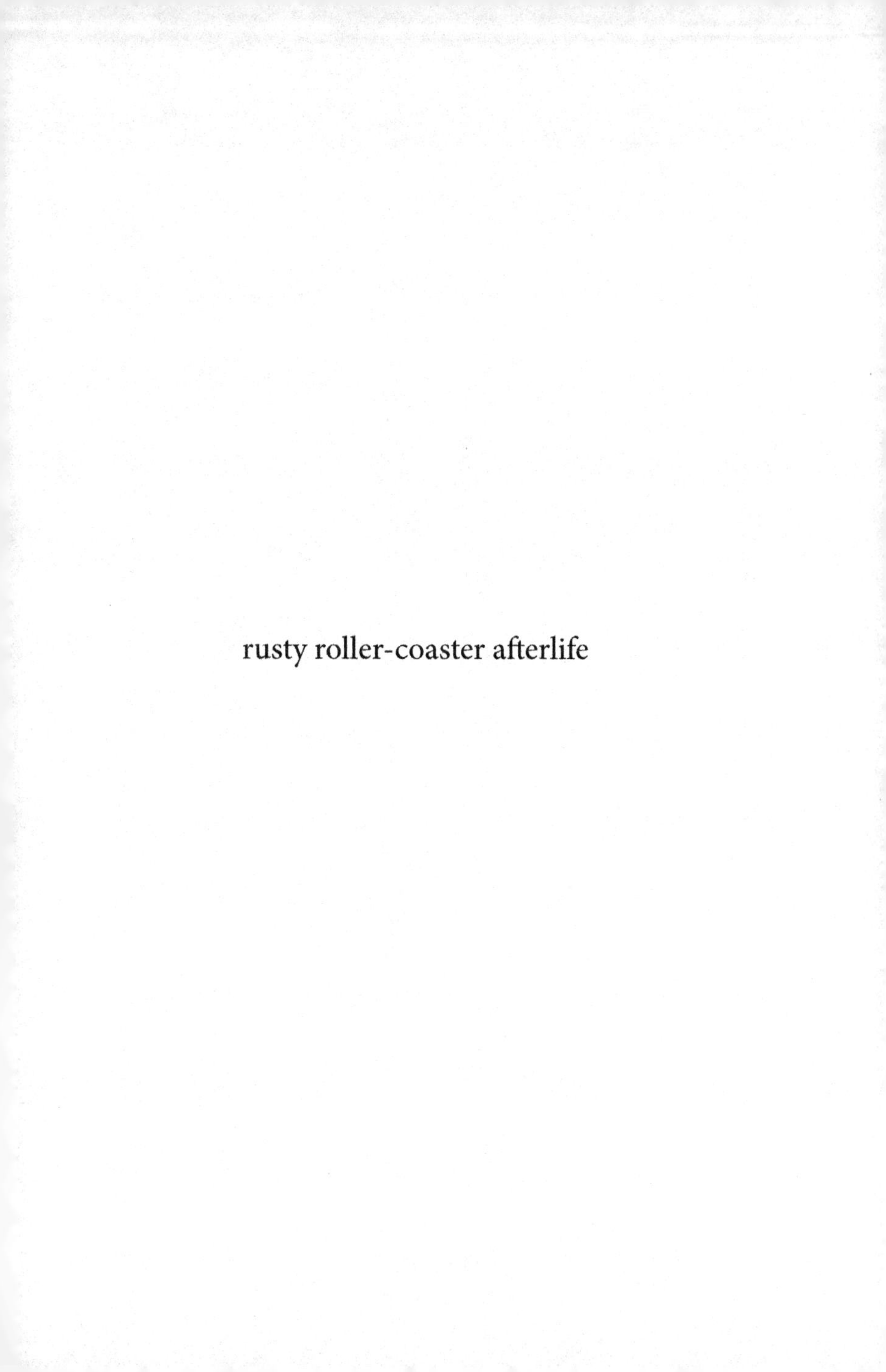

rusty roller-coaster afterlife

HOLOGRAM OFFICE

Simplicity and truth are close relatives. A thing that is not true must be proven repeatedly.

a majority of mockingbirds

NATURE / NURTURE

We've already talked about life after death. Both think
it unlikely. Neither of us knows.

With dictionaries in our laps — me in my kitchen, Bob
in the hospice dayroom, we are trying to see if there is
a common root between the words "numinous" and
"numismatic." Though they look similar and, at least
in my dictionary, appear one right after the other, we
can find no direct relationship.

> a full nest
> one of them
> the cowbird egg

another haiku about a mockingbird

small town
the same dream
as last night

my shadow
in wet
cement

summer ending mostly painted house

mint condition
an autumn day
still in the wrapper

a blonde, a brunette
and a redhead
leaf viewing

cottonwood seeds drift
through the empty parking lot
a new mass shooting

more automatic words about weapons

talking to my dog
I explain
the election

the way we left our dining room chairs

at the airport
my anxiety
takes off

POSTMAN

The playing cards are soft and pliant, damp and gritty from long days of solitaire. He has been retired for eleven years.

yes colored maybe

midnight where my keys are

no
end
of
not
enough

collabor tion

cold start
days of writing
the wrong date

stooped
over the sink
another year

skipping stone
the pond
iced over

the
of
winter

my cat
content to let me
do the talking

sleep
a layer deeper
snow

expecting
no one
arrives

winter night
the outside
of a door

tomorrow

tomorrow

GRANNY

Her death is the death I want. She seemed to simply wear out. An hour before, she was laughing with me about how she was reaching out to a hallucination. Or was it?

> light
> and the question
> of light

young river—
the cataracts
and minor falls

riding shotgun
in the sportscar
a sapling

with us
as with migrant birds
a reprise
of certain songs
and certain places

around the corner
walking her
oxygen tank

that water in a glass in the water feeling

both of all
naked as
the under sun

gone from
the shady spot
his Chevy pickup

well beyond
a loving touch
into hands
whose quality
is expertise

as if there's to be
an eleventh commandment,
the moon breaks through clouds

what's in it
for me
refrigerator light

LOGIC

It seems to me there's a difference between the pleasure of solving one or two Sudoku puzzles in a daily newspaper and solving one of many in a pocket book entirely devoted to them.

    public beach
    the attention due
    to a wave

her soup making
fills the apartment
autumn evening

Indian summer
my lunch
under the heat lamp

home from college
she disapproves of
the new drapes

might have snubbed me but for their dog

first snow
the spare key
beneath a rock

actor
in a family
of critics

no longer the athlete I never was

music lesson
the teacher practices
patience

her blue
his red
and never quite
the right shade
of violet

November dusk
invitations
from the crows

autumn traveler
no one who saw me today
will see me again

a tune
in the shepherd's head
sung by wolves

late for the Zen lecture
        most of the time
            I am missing nothing

lift a pencil
the poem
floats away

MILIEU

It's everything that precedes us on what appears to be
a bare stage.

>opening
>night
>a
>full
>moon

It's who owns the theatre and what they expect of
us. It's the "regular" audience and how we seem in
light of what they've previously experienced. It's the
impression made on those who are here for the first
time. If we've had a chance to rehearse here, it's how
those rehearsals have gone. It's the weaving of moods
among people filing in, through the lobby and stage
doors. Our performances, as actors and as audience,
are even affected by where we anticipate going after
the show. Cleveland, perhaps.

>the mountain
>across the lake
>a shimmer

untouched snow
our imaginary
relationship

first love
both of us learning
to ice skate

calving the winter moon fjord

finding within
the gestures
of winter trees

snow has made a coffin of a stone bench

canned peaches
the darkest corner
of the cellar

the snow
leading
by example

someone
we can trust
with winter

SINCE I HAVE RETIRED . . .

the sensation of time has changed for me. Once,
like wire strung between anchored points, it had the
pluck and twang of a banjo string. Now it's like rope.
Sometimes tied to something, though never with
much tension. And sometimes just hanging loose in
my hand.

    another school year
    certain trees turn
    before the others

maple taps catching winter sun

mitten on the path
everything now
belongs to spring

mason jar
half full
of tadpoles

willow
thy will
be done

cherry-blossom rain
ready or not
I am a father

Mother's Day morning
one child knows the formula
for coffee

VOORHIES HILL

My best friend through childhood and adolescence was one of twelve siblings, falling somewhere in the middle. His family lived on a farm, from which they drew subsistence and little more. The family was proud. Some were prouder than others.

birth certificate
an honorable
mention

give a penny
take a penny
1948

the soldiers drift in
a few at a time
Arlington

mid-summer
where I'd be
if I had traveled

pulling weeds—
the angry back
of her knees

leaving
the body—
snakeskin

shoes
at the bottom
of the slide

the camera's small eye on the mountain

heavy Buddha
resting briefly
on the sofa

classic rock
the grey portion
of his soul patch

THE RULE OF ME

As applied to highway driving, it goes like this: anyone driving more slowly is a dangerous idiot, creating a hazard for normal drivers, and anyone driving faster is just a homicidal maniac.

> drinking straw
> and rapier
> a hummingbird

in the background
someone else
taking a selfie

second day
in the guest room
an extension cord

lonely
having the best
memory

one last comment on simplicity

apparently all there is windows

Prior Publication Credits

Some of this work previously appeared in:

Acorn
American Tanka
Close to the Wind (2013 H.N.A. Anthology)
ColoradoBlvd.net
Frameless Sky
Frogpond
Hudson Valley Haiku-kai
is/let
Kernels
Mariposa
Modern Haiku
Ribbons
Seabeck 2017 Anthology
Sketchbook
Upstate Dim Sum
Vancouver Cherry Blossom Festival

John Stevenson was born in Ithaca, New York and currently lives in the village of Nassau, New York. He is a former president of the Haiku Society of America (2000), former editor of its literary journal, *Frogpond* (2005 – 2007) and current managing editor of *The Heron's Nest* (since 2008). He is also the current (2018 – 2019) honorary curator of the American Haiku Archives at the California State Library. His other haiku collections include *Something Unerasable* (1995), *Some of the Silence* (1999), *Quiet Enough* (2004), *Live Again* (2009), and *d(ark)* (2014). The final four titles are Red Moon Press publications.

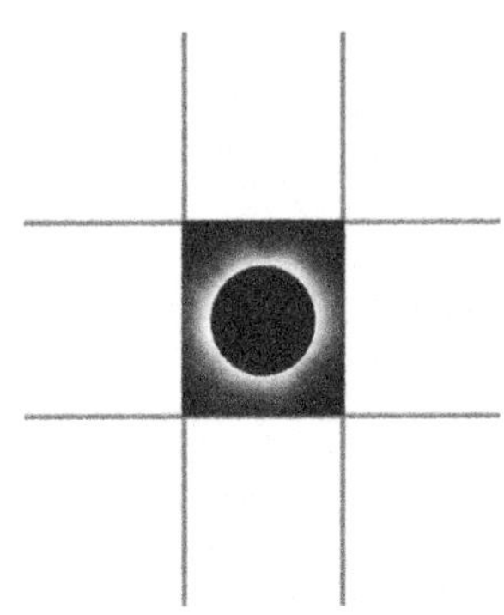

Made in the USA
Monee, IL
07 July 2026

56644832R00059